Millionaire Mindset Now!

Think Yourself to Wealth

Ben Garcia

Copyright © 2019 Ben Garcia

All rights reserved.

ISBN: 9781796981315

CONTENTS

	Preface	i
	Introduction	iii
Chapter 1	Being a Millionaire Is Possible	1
Chapter 2	How to Reprogram Your Mindset Now!	13
Chapter 3	Goals!	37
Chapter 4	Create a Plan	49
Chapter 5	Your Greatest Asset	59
Chapter 6	Don't Work For Money	63
Chapter 7	Self-Discipline	69
Chapter 8	Enemies of Success	77
Chapter 9	Do Now!	89

PREFACE

I wrote this book nearly a year ago. I had the book cover designed and the context professionally edited. I could have had a million reasons why I didn't go through all the way with it and have it published. But the real reason (or better yet, the excuse) I didn't have it published is because I WAS AFRAID. Of what? I'm not sure. Maybe it was fear of failure or fear of other people's opinions. It doesn't matter. The facts were plain. I had a vision. A vision of a book. And I went all the way to the cusp of executing all the goals and action steps to make that vision a reality except the final one. Which was have it published and release it to the world.

I was in the shower one morning and it dawned on me: Why would I write that book? It was clearly on my heart to spend the time, money and energy creating it. It was my passion to add value to people. I set a goal and I shied away from it. I broke my own word to myself. Not only that but I've in effect broken my word to everyone it would possibly effect, and also, I've broken my word to God, my friends and my family. So that very day I sat down proofread, reviewed and finalized the book. I added this preface, formatted it and published it. Here it is.

Whether one person or a million people read this, it doesn't matter. All that matters is I mustered up the courage and did it even in the face of fear. That's what life's all about. That's success…

INTRODUCTION

I want to see you succeed. I wrote this book to equip you for success. Society, parenting, the school system, and all other false voices have equipped us for failure. I'm not saying they did this on purpose. But "it's just how it's been," so that's what they taught you, me, and everyone else in America.

If you're offended by that, then, hey, if you want to live a nice "comfortable" life with a "good" job, making an average salary, with your "dream" car, living the American (MIDDLE CLASS!) dream, and probably enslaved to debt, your boss, and the government for the rest of your life, then by all means go for it and stop reading this book right now.

This book is not for those who want to live average or "comfortable" lives. This book is for those who want to succeed and succeed BIG. This book is for those who won't take average for an answer and who want to ultimately change the world. Even if you just want to make a lot of money, this book is for you.

CHAPTER 1
BEING A MILLIONAIRE IS POSSIBLE

CAN I BE SUCCESSFUL? This is the first question you may be asking yourself, and the answer is: Yes! Absolutely 100%! This is the first step for the successful few and the last step for the unsuccessful many. Many people do not succeed because they think they cannot succeed—at least not at tremendous levels—and therefore they settle for less, or they settle for someone else's definition of success. Most of America's ideal view of success is having a good job, going in debt for a good house and a good car, and having a good life: a.k.a. the "American Dream."

These things can seem good, and that's because they are the average person's idea of success... Did you notice what I just said there? They are the AVERAGE person's idea. Are you average? No, I don't think so. I don't know you personally, but I know that you are not average. And you should therefore not settle for an average cash flow, average net worth, average investments, or a plain Jane, average life. If you have any doubt about you not being average, please take the time to read the next few pages. I'm pleading with you, you've got to hear this. It's imperative to your future.

Wealth is a Way of Thinking

The rich are wealthy because their minds have been conditioned to think, and therefore act, in a certain way. This is absolutely essential to understand. The reason why so many people fail to take full advantage and completely embrace their potential of success and wealth generation is because they are limited by invisible barriers that are set up within their brains. Their mindset, or mental model, has been put together over their infant through adolescent years growing up from what they've been told and experienced. Their paradigm of how the world works is practically an accumulation of what they've been told is true and what is false. They also have learned "how things are" through personal experiences. So, when we fail once in a particular area, we assume we are a complete failure in that area: so why even try again? This is our go-to reasoning for failure, and it is false reasoning.

There are so many false beliefs and myths that we grow up believing. Such as, there is a shortage of success or money, we are only capable of so much, we aren't good enough, we must go into debt to go to college, we have to settle for the best job we can get with our degree, following our dreams is unrealistic (obviously!), and much, much more.

We've grown up hearing things from our parents like "money doesn't grow on trees," "I'm not made of money," or "that's not how the world works." We have also heard other things like "be careful" or "calm down" when we were younger and begin to believe that having a high level of energy, enthusiasm, and ambition is not normal, good, or healthy. (When in fact it is healthy, or else why would you be born with those innate characteristics?)

Do you remember asking your parents why about something and their response was "because I said so"? Yes, exactly. It's because they said so that you now have a limited understanding of your potential, your ability, and how to act. (Yes, how you think 100% effects how you act; you only act in a certain way because you think in a certain way.) Okay, so your parents told you so. And who told them so? Their parents? And who told their parents so? Your great-grandparents? Come on! Of course, your great-grandparents told them that. The biggest experiences they ever had with money and how the world works were during the Great Depression of the 1930s. And even still, your great grandparents were poor then while Henry Ford and thousands of other multimillionaires weren't just surviving, they were thriving because they understood how money works, they understood the tricks of the trade, and they understood success! Besides all that, that was an entirely different age, this is the information age—the future! Opportunity to succeed and make lots and lots of money has never been so available to the general public—the average Joe—than ever before! And you and I aren't average at all, so we should be massive successes.

This limitation also especially effects our understanding of how money works and how to get it. Most were raised being told that they had to work hard for money. Did you know that the rich think the exact opposite? They understand the main way of getting money is by having money work hard for you!

Throw Away Your Old Thought Patterns Now!

I'm going to get a little deep here for a second, so bear with me. As a human being, you are made up of three parts: a body, soul, and spirit. Your body is simply your physical form—it only lives for so long; it needs oxygen, food, and water to live; and eventually, it dies away. Your spirit is the real you that lives on after your body dies away. Your soul consists of your mind, will, and emotions. This is your consciousness and personality. It evolves and changes over time and determines what you DO in the physical world via your body. This is your soul, or your mind, will, and emotions at work. You feel a certain way (emotions), which causes you to think a certain way (mind), which ultimately causes you to act a certain way (will).

You must get rid of the old, faulty, conditioned thinking of the poor and middle-class. You must develop and assume a correct view of your potential, success, and money. That's what the Millionaire Mindset Now! is all about. You can have the mindset of a millionaire, and you can have it now! This is essentially changing your self-image and your paradigm of how the world works.

The number one way to get rid of old thought patterns (i.e., habits) is by replacing them with new thought patterns. By new, I also mean correct patterns which are in harmony with what you are truly capable of. I want you to understand that you really are capable of infinite accomplishment. Whatever you set your mind to you can achieve. It seems cliché, but it really is true. You have no limits. The only limits you have are the limits in your mind. You allow these limits in your mind, and since you've allowed them in, you can kick them out as well. The world and everyone around you have placed invisible limits on you that your mind then accepts as true. Most of these limits are subconscious, and you really have to dive deep to see they are there. Once you find one or more, you must destroy them quickly. They are your enemy. They are telling you what you can and cannot do, and most of these beliefs are based on false information that has no factual basis.

Ask yourself these questions:

- How do I think about a particular subject (money, success, my abilities, etc.)?

- Why do I think this way about this particular subject?

- What limiting beliefs to I have about this subject?

- Are these beliefs based off of solid facts?

- Has anything else I have observed (e.g., success people) proven these unreal beliefs to be contradictory to my understanding of reality?

The Destiny Mindset

Millionaires and other successful people understand that it is their destiny to be successful. This conviction (more about convictions in the next chapter) drives them, in fact, it compels them toward success. You have to believe that it is your destiny to be successful. Because it really is. You have to ingrain this deep into your subconscious mind.

All things are possible. You are unique. You have a right—a duty—to give it all you got. You can and will be successful (just follow the steps in this book). You are a storehouse of pure potential. No one of these 7 and a half billion people on planet earth have thought like you, talked like you, or acted like you. No one has had your experiences or has had your opportunity, nor will anyone ever. No one has had your dreams, ambitions, and visions of the future and what the future could, should, and can be like. No one can make an impact like you or in such a way as you. No one ever before, now or in the future has ever lived your life: and no one ever will. You are divinely different from everyone else for a reason. For such a time as this! This is your chance.

Don't you want to be like one of "the Greats"? Well, what if I told you that you are one of the Greats? Even though you may not see yourself that way now, it is because it is now, and the future is forward in time. Infinite opportunity lays before your path. The Greats were and are people just like you. What set them apart was not luck or some special, magical gift, talent or ability they had (although that did play a part, you have gifts, talents, and abilities as well!), it was the fact that they saw their destiny before them and instead of passively letting life go by, they decided to embrace all they were created to be and thus changed the world. You can do that as well, and I know you will because you are Great! There are 3 types of "Greats": The Greats of yesterday, today, and tomorrow. You can be one of the Greats of tomorrow, but you must choose today. You must choose now!

"The empires of the future are the empires of the mind."

Winston Churchill

You were created and placed at this place and this time for a reason. Wherever you are right now, it's for a purpose. If you don't like where you are, it may be your time and season to move into a more appropriate place and take on a new venture. You may have dreams and desires to become a millionaire and be really successful. Fortunately for you, today, it is easier and more possible to become a massive success than at any other time in history. Technology and information have so far advanced that to not be successful is almost a disgrace to yourself as a human being, to the founding fathers of this great, opportunistic free country, to your fellow human beings and society, and to God who created you with a purpose. You literally insult everyone else in the world when you CHOOSE not to succeed.

Success is a choice. Being a millionaire is a choice. Being a multimillionaire is a choice. Being a billionaire is a choice. You must choose to be what you want to be. No one else is going to choose for you, and if you decide to not choose, then you disappear with the rest of the no-names of yesteryear. Who are the no-names? I don't know. No one knows, that's why they are no-names. They chose to fail. Choosing to not win is choosing to fail. Plain and simple.

> *"Whether you think you can or you can't, you're right."*
>
> Henry Ford

The future you is hanging in front of you. Choose success, matter of fact, choose massive success! You are capable of massive success. There is no shortage of success or money. History has proven this to be true time and time again. Was there a shortage of success for Napoleon, Sir Isaac Newton, Albert Einstein, Thomas Edison, Henry Ford, Andrew Carnegie, Alexander Graham Bell, Warren Buffet, Bill Gates, or Steve Jobs? You might be thinking, "Well that was back in the day when there weren't that many advances, and of course, things like the telephone, electricity, motor vehicles, and computers were bound to come out." What?! Of course, they were bound to come out, because there were people who saw the world how it was and saw what it needed and decided to fill in the blanks with their ideas, products, and services. These people had a destiny, and they embraced it. There were probably people before them whose destiny was to do what those people ended up doing, but because they chose not to embrace their destiny, their potential was squandered, and their success never came to pass and was buried with them in their grave. (What a sad story!)

There were people thinking just like you back in those times: "Oh, this is as far as we are going to advance. Why would we need metal horses when we have real horses, or lightbulbs when we have candles? And sending a person's voice across the world via electricity through wires? Come on, that's nonsense!" Yeah, we all saw how thinking like that worked out for those people: you don't even know who they are. Then there is the whole idea of "you must be a genius to come up with any world-changing invention." False! These "visionaries and geniuses" were just like you, as human beings, they just thought differently—

their mindset was different. Where people saw limitations, they saw opportunity. Now, I'm not saying you have to invent some crazy, future-altering innovation or start some super-innovative, visionary company like Amazon or Microsoft to be a massive success; I'm just pointing out that those people were just like you. They just chose to be who they desired to be. The same goes for multimillionaires. You can be a multimillionaire. It's not as complicated as everyone thinks. You must destroy those barriers of "complications" in order to become a millionaire, multimillionaire, or even billionaire.

Morgan Freeman once said something in a movie that hit me like a brick, he said, "Insanity is coasting through life in a miserable existence when you have a caged lion locked inside and the key to release it." You have a purpose and destiny. It's only a matter of discovering it and then acting on it—working it out. Life isn't about determining your future, but I believe it is about finding your passion, dream, and vision of your future and the future of humanity that is innate in you from birth and combine that with your gifts, talents, and abilities to make that vision go from abstract to reality. You'll know what it is because you'll know in your knower—your inner being, down to your core—that this is what you were created to do and be.

The first thing necessary for assuming and gaining the Millionaire Mindset Now! is to figure out what it is you want. It can be anything. Take the time right now to think about what it is that you really want. Not what somebody else wants for you, but what you want. It doesn't even have to be money, it can be anything. Like I said, you'll know what it is. It's a matter of self-exploration. For example, if it's to be a multimillionaire, why do you want to be a multimillionaire? Maybe so you could start philanthropic work in North Africa. Okay, why do you want to do that? And keep asking these questions until you get to the root of what it is you really want. During this exercise, assume there are no limitations on what you can do (because there really isn't any limits to your ability). If you could do or achieve anything in the world, what would you want to do or achieve?

"If we did all the things we were capable of doing, we would literally astonish ourselves."

Thomas Edison

CHAPTER 2
HOW TO REPROGRAM YOUR MINDSET NOW!

It's essential that you come to the realization that you really are capable of infinite achievement. You have no limitations. This saying is 100% true: Whatever you set your mind to you can achieve. Of course, there must be a proportionate amount of planning, effort, and action needed to have your dreams and goals realized. Nevertheless, whatever you desire is possible.

There's no such thing as impossible. I've seen the impossible manifest into the possible in my life and the lives of others, and it blows logical thinking out the water. It's beyond anything of this world, it is literally spiritual. What's even more powerful about it is when you see it come to pass from abstract to concrete your faith is boosted even higher, and your confidence goes to levels out of this world, and you are able to succeed more and more and at higher and more unreal levels. This phenomenon is why winners keep winning. It's the Law of Inertia at work—the forces of everything around you—working towards your good and favor. This is faith + perseverance + goals. When you really believe something, and you set goals and continue to persevere with an intense focus towards your goals with immense action, eventually you will achieve your goals no matter what. (I speak explicitly about the power of goal setting and how to effectively set goals in the next chapter.)

The (Scary) Potential of Your Subconscious Mind

If you do not know what I mean when I say the subconscious mind, then let me take a moment to explain. You have two minds: a conscious and a subconscious. Your conscious mind is what you use when you're actively using your mind. For example, when you are actively trying to solve a problem, you are consciously working it out: you are aware of it. Now, you can also be subconsciously solving a problem. Well, what do you mean, Ben? I mean have you ever been trying to solve a problem, let's say you've been at it all day and it's driving you crazy. Even while you're lying in bed at night, it's keeping you up. So, you pop a melatonin or Benadryl and finally pass out. The next morning you wake up and "Aha!" You've figured out the problem you were trying to solve. You think, "Crap, it must've been those drugs I took last night. I need to start taking those more often." No! This is your subconscious mind at work, baby. It's always at work.

Your subconscious mind never sleeps. While you're sitting around, even while you're working, your subconscious mind's gears are turning and churning. (Now that by no means gives you an excuse to work less or less hard! It should make you want to work harder because this is multiplying your efficiency, productivity, and overall impact in all spheres of your life—this is the epidemy of compound interest at work.) Whatever has been planted in your subconscious mind, whether intentionally or not, is being broke down, analyzed, put back together, and broken down all over again and again. It solves problems and creates new ones. It is the backbone of all your decisions, whether you believe it or not.

Your subconscious is also where your self-image abides. Your self-image is your image of yourself and all that you are and believe. Your self-image is how you view yourself (this is extremely important). It is developed and constantly evolving via accumulation of emotions, thoughts, past experiences, and self-talk. I get more into this later in the chapter, until then let's take a second to go through this example of how your subconscious mind works in a situation:

You meet Jeff for the first time, and his eyes are bug-eyed and constantly looking around you during your conversation with him. You "know" that probably means he's not interested in you or he is rude, so you file away that assumption. Your subconscious mind takes that assumption and from here on out assumes Jeff is not interested in you and decides that you aren't very fond of Jeff and that he is not to be trusted. Now, on the conscious level, you are completely unaware of this subconscious assumption's power. You've brushed it off, it was no big deal anyway, stuff like that happens all the time, right? Months later, your good friend Sarah is totally crushing on Jeff and expresses her feeling towards him to you. Your first response is "eh." She counters, "What's wrong with him? He's cute, nice and cool: the full package!" (*wink, wink*) You say, "I don't know... I've always had a bad feeling about that guy. I don't trust him is all." So, Sarah decides to agree with your analysis because she both consciously and subconsciously trusts you and forgets the feelings she has for him.

Okay, so you just ruined a potentially amazing couple. This could have been the best thing for both Jeff and Sarah's life. All because why? You don't like Jeff? But, why? What has Jeff ever done to you? Nothing, but your subconscious mind was working against you. Yes, your subconscious mind can work against you, and it does a surprising majority of your life. And having your subconscious mind work against you is the reason why most people never live up to their full potential. Because their subconscious minds have been programmed to enslave them to the false beliefs that the world (everything and everyone else), and even their own minds, have fed it.

This is ancient instincts at work trying to protect you against future risks. In tribal times, you probably would have saved Sarah and your tribe from being raped, slaughtered, and plundered. But in this century, I don't think Jeff would have done any of that. For God's sake, Jeff is afraid to invest in anything more than index mutual funds, much less have the audacity to hurt, much less kill anyone! What, forget jail. Jeff has to keep his cubicle job paying $56,000 salary. He'll lose all his benefits and company-matched 401k that he's worked so hard for! He may even have to pull another mortgage out on his house he can't afford. How will he do that when he's got that $20,000 overdue balance on his four credit cards, you may be wondering? I don't know but don't you even dare remind him about his car loan he's upside-down on. (Wait, where was I? Sorry!)

Come on! You don't want your subconscious mind working against you. Why would you want to be your own biggest enemy? You want to be your biggest ally! It's time to get your subconscious mind to get on the same level of thinking as the future you—the destined, Great you. It's time to get that thing to start working in your favor. Luckily, there's a way to get that ball rolling, and to get it rolling now!

> *Jesus knew their thoughts and said to them: "Any kingdom divided against itself will be ruined, and a house divided against itself will fall."*
>
> Luke 11:17

Destiny Affirmation

Do you feel stuck? This feeling of being stuck is simply you constantly thinking the same way and creating the same experiences again and again. It's the very definition of insanity! The only way to get out of this rut is to think differently and act differently. Instead of thinking "I cannot get out of this circumstance," think "I can," set goals to determine where you want to go, begin coming up with creative ways to get out, and then act on those plans.

If you're not convinced of your infinite potential, I have a practical exercise to help you renew your mind. I call this exercise destiny affirmation. I do this exercise myself every single day, sometimes multiple times a day. It is done by simply writing down positively-affirming statements about yourself and repeating them in the first-person, present tense. It's preferable to say these statements out loud. When you take just a few minutes out of your day to repeat these statements to yourself, it gets deep-rooted into your subconscious mind and therefore holds itself continually at the forefront of your mind throughout the day. You then, begin to act out these characteristics and behavior. Eventually, it holds itself at the forefront of your mind forever. Yes, you can be forever confident and successful.

> *"Death and life are in the power of the tongue, and those who love it will eat its fruit."*
>
> Proverbs 18:21

This is the power of your words being worked out. Words are far more powerful than people realize. Have you known someone who has been verbally abused or bullied? These people begin to believe the statements they're constantly told. Someone, like their parent or spouse, tells them "You will never amount to anything" or "you're a failure." These are harsh, destructive statements, and the worst thing about them is that they are false. No one is a failure. Neither you nor anyone else can fail at being a person. People can only fail at reaching their full potential and, instead, settle for less than they are capable of. (But that's not you, right?) These people are not failures, but they have been conditioned, no, convinced rather, that they are failures or that they are only good for so much. This is not only detrimental to the person's level of success in life but also their health. This destroys mental health and can even cause physical health issues and possibly eat away at them to the point of premature physical death. Yes, that is how much of an impact words have on people.

Even if one person is "just joking," it hurts in both the short-term and the long-term. If they say, "no worries, I didn't take it personally," don't believe it, because their subconscious mind is definitely taking it personally. (Now, you can thwart negative statements or assumptions, of course, but first you must be trained in the true, positive affirmations about yourself so that you can identify the false, negative suggestions, and therefore use your conscious mind to reject it from being accepted by your subconscious mind.) Neither you nor anyone else has the right to tell someone what they cannot do. If someone ever tells you that you cannot do something, get as far away from that person as possible. They will suck the life out of you, I promise.

No one likes being told negative things. Every single person wants to be encouraged, regardless of if they say differently. People want positive affirmation that is congruent with who they really are and what they really are capable of. Even if in pride they reject it or out of humility disregard it, they want to know that they matter. It's because they do matter, but they are constantly beaten down by circumstances, other people, and their own minds (emotions, such as fear, doubt, and any other negative self-talk). Deep down inside we all want warm words of love and encouragement. Without it, we fade away and become a negative, pessimistic mess.

So, why would we want to keep telling ourselves negative things? It's because we've grown up that way. We've been told by our parents (with good intention) to "get out of the street!", "what were you thinking?", "What's wrong with you? You could've hurt yourself!" and so on, but they only told us half the story. They forgot to say the reason behind their angry outburst and rigid rules, which was that they love you, they want you around a long time, so you could grow up and live a long and happy life, they want to see you succeed. In school, our teacher put x's next to the questions we got wrong but not checks next to the ones we got right. Our whole life, everything we got wrong was emphasized, whereas everything we got right was ignored. These things are stored in our subconscious and transferred to our paradigm, which stays with us through our adult years. We make a big deal of our failures and minimize the value of our successes when this should be the exact opposite. This type of thinking eats away and essentially crushes our self-esteem and devalues our self-image. The end result is poor self-esteem and low confidence (how we think and feel), which translates into poor performance and low success rates (how we act).

We talk to ourselves negatively all the time. Psychologists estimate that about 80% of our self-talk is negative. You may be thinking that you don't think that way. Oh, but you do. When you say things like "I can't afford it," "that's not possible," "I'm tired," "I'm sick," "I don't know," "I can't," "I shouldn't have done that," "I'm an idiot for saying that," and on and on. Those are all negative things you are telling yourself. Don't say "you can't afford it," rather ask "how can I afford it?" Rather than, "I don't know," how about "I'll figure out" and instead of "I can't" how about "I can!" Because you definitely can!

You might be thinking you have to worry about guarding every thought you think. Now that you are aware of the power of negative thoughts, you're creating more negative thoughts through fear and worry! Just because you're having negative thoughts doesn't mean you have to work night and day guarding and filtering every single thought because that would drive you completely insane, wouldn't it? The good news is that it has been scientifically proven that a positive thought is hundreds of times more powerful than a negative thought! Therefore, every time you speak positive affirmations over yourself and your life you practically cancel out a hundred negative thoughts.

> *"You do not believe what you see; you see what you believe."*
>
> Wayne Dyre

It doesn't really matter if what you believe is true or false. Your subconscious mind doesn't know anything outside of what your conscious mind tells it. If you believe it's true, then it's true for you. If you tell your subconscious mind that something is right, then it believes it is right. Your subconscious mind is the dwelling place of your self-image and your paradigm (or understanding) of outside reality. Therefore, you're better off believing positive, success-making, destiny-affirming facts. When you constantly feed your subconscious mind with destiny affirmations, you are building convictions. These are strongholds in your mind, and they are the basis of many of your habits. (Habits are formed when a certain amount of your neurons has been conditioned into thinking a certain way, thus forming a neurological pattern, or stronghold. The good news is that, whether they are good or bad habits, they can be changed because of the neuroplasticity of your mind. Habits were formed using neuroplasticity, and they can be changed or removed in the same way.) A conviction is a strong belief or value. Thought plus emotion creates conviction, and conviction creates reality. When you have a strong conviction (for example, high levels of self-confidence), your subconscious mind makes it evident through the way you carry yourself. It can literally be seen shining in your eyes.

If you have low self-esteem, everyone you talk to can pick it up, whether consciously or subconsciously, they'll know, because the tone of your voice, your posture and gesticulations (or lack thereof), and low energy are byproducts of a weak or false conviction. When you believe firmly about something and have a passionate, real belief about it, people see it and are drawn to it. Your subconscious mind only considers those things that your conscious mind tells it to be true. The outside reality of the world does not shift or change according to your subconscious thoughts and beliefs. What happens is your subconscious mind filters out all the information it receives from the outside world (reality) to fit what the conscious mind has told it to be true. That's why it's so pointless to try to prove someone wrong because they will always think they are right. Even if you are right, their subconscious mind believes otherwise, and unless their conscious mind informs their subconscious minds of the contrary via constant self-talk about it, they will not believe it.

"As a man thinketh in his heart, so is he"
Proverbs 23:7

Here's an example of a few of my dream affirmations I repeat to myself on a daily basis:

- I am hyper-intentional, laser-focused, attentive, alert and fully at the moment at every given moment.

- I am a happy, positive, and energetic person.

- I am bold and courageous!

- I am confident, charismatic, and powerful.

- I am blessed and highly favored!

- I assume complete responsibility for myself and for everything that happens to me.

- I am a winner.

- I see opportunities that others miss.

- Creativity flows through me.

- I'm obligated to strive for and thereby reap MASSIVE amounts of success because I am capable and destined to do so. IT IS

MY CALLING AND PURPOSE.

- I was born to achieve all my goals; it is my responsibility—my duty!

Did you notice how I wrote my destiny affirmations? They are in the first-person, present tense. There's something extremely powerful in saying these destiny affirmations to your mind in the first-person, present tense. Your mind assumes them and believes them to be true. Eventually, they become true, because your subconscious mind is working in your favor. Whenever you've achieved what you constantly thought of (whether positive or negative), was because you used your conscious mind to choose your desirable you and influenced your subconscious mind to be your ally and start working with you, not against you.

Another thing is to avoid words like "no," "not," or "never." Your subconscious mind does not know the difference between negative and positive words and statements, it only hears positive. So, when you consciously affirm to yourself "I will never be poor," your subconscious mind hears "I will be poor," and thus it makes sure, with your cooperation, that this becomes a reality.

That was just a taste of a few of my personal destiny affirmations. I have many more. I'm sure you have a good idea of how you would like yours by now. I want you to take the time right now and write some down. If you're having trouble thinking of some, then think of the leaders and successful people that you aspire to be. Think of the qualities that make them stand apart from the rest of the crowd. Think of the characteristics that they display which you desire to have. Do you want to be confident? Fearless? Unshakeable? Analytical? Super intentional? What is it you want to be? Even if you have some of that, you could always use more. Write it down right now. I challenge you not to read any further until you have written at least ten destiny affirmations. And do not go today or tomorrow without repeating them. Make it a habit. You know how they say it takes 21 days to make something a habit? Well, start doing it now and for however many days until it is a habit. Then, do not stop doing it ever. If you are determined and put in the effort, you will reach success.

The key is that we change from the inside out! We become what we think about most. If we focus on negative thoughts, then negative things tend to happen. If we focus on positive thoughts, positive things tend to come our way. If we think we are poor, we stay poor. If you obsess over all the things that could go wrong, it'll probably all go wrong. "What I feared has come upon me; what I dreaded has happened to me" (Job 3:25). To quote Shakespeare in

Hamlet Act 2, Scene 2: "there is nothing either good or bad, but thinking makes it so." Is it any wonder that when the news is making a giant deal about the flu when it comes to that time of the year that everybody suddenly gets sick with the flu? If everyone wasn't talking, worrying, and fearing getting the flu, they might have never got it themselves. But since they dwell over it and it overtakes their minds, it becomes inevitable that they should get the flu, right?

The same principle happens when we think about health and wealth. When a strong desire or focus is mixed with large amounts of emotion, our subconscious minds creatively make ways to reach the goal of that desire or focus. The physical equivalent of our intangible goals and desires literally seem to be attracted to us. This is because our positive, destiny-affirming thoughts attract like thoughts and when our minds are infected with positive destiny-affirming mindset, we are thrust into action, and we begin using the power of our subconscious minds to develop creative plans and solutions combined with energy and action and attain what we focus on.

Dream Conjuring

"All thoughts which have been emotionalized (given feeling) and mixed with faith (expectancy), begin immediately to translate themselves into their physical equivalent."

Napoleon Hill

There are a million things out there about positive thinking and the law of attraction that are all great resources (mostly repetitive), but what I'm trying to teach you is something that transcends just a positive mental attitude. Now I believe in many aspects of the law of attraction and other similar ideas. However, I don't believe you just visualize and believe in a better future and sit back and think you will passively attract money and success. That violates other laws. You cannot violate a law with another law unless one or the other is not actually a law. The Law of Attraction states that likes attract likes, which is true. With our thoughts, we attract more of the same thoughts, and thoughts translate into action. But thinking at certain "frequencies" does not literally attract physical things to us. We are not gods. We can create things in our minds, but we cannot change the physical word with abstract thoughts. We can only change the physical with the physical. However, the root is in our minds, which is why the way we think is so critical to the process of shaping our lives.

There is a greater law at work which is the Universal Law of Cause and Effect, otherwise known as "you reap what you sow." This is of biblical origin but ask any successful (or even unsuccessful) business person and they will agree. The Law of Cause and Effect is a law: if you sow positive, you reap positive, and if you sow negative, you reap negative. You don't plant corn and expect a wheat harvest. That isn't how the universe works. Jesus said it best, "A good tree cannot bear bad fruit, and a bad tree cannot bear good fruit" (Matthew 7:18). If you are getting bad fruit (undesirable results), then the cause is most likely at the root of the tree (your thinking). Laziness is never rewarded with anything other than the consequences of inaction and slothfulness. You cannot steal or cheat your way to the top. Those at the top worked hard, smart, and with laser focus and determination. There is no shortcut to success.

What I'm inferring to is something I call Dream Conjuring. It is the process of bringing your dream (which is yet to have been realized) from abstract to concrete—to the point of realization. Think of it as the materialization of your vision from intangible to tangible or summoning your mental picture of your ideal future from imagination to reality. Using your mind's eye to visualize what you have not yet attained kickstarts your subconscious mind into a rapid mode of processing, planning, and problem-solving. There is a vision, a goal, an objective; and your mind has set its course to that desired destination. Once the mind is set and focused at a fixed point it aspires to reach, it can begin the process of planning. Until there is a destination or target, you're just going through life on autopilot. With no future ambitions, you're just sailing with the wind—not steering your ship in an intentional and calculated way. "It's all about the process," the enlightened hipster says, "you got to experience the journey, man." Of course, you experience the journey. But there is no journey if there is no destination. "Going with the flow" of life is not a journey; that's a wasted life.

> *"You are a living magnet. What you attract into your life is in harmony with your dominant thoughts."*
>
> Brian Tracy

Now, I want you to imagine what you want your future to look like. Go all out, assume there are no limits to what you can do. Now, what does it look like? Envision every detail. How do you want your financial situation to look like? (I want you to actually picture numbers in your bank account.) How about your love life and other relationships? How big of an impact do you want to make? Come on! I want you to actually close your eyes and visualize the future that you want. In your visualizations, see, in detail, what you want, the life your living in the first person—from your point of view. Now, feel the emotions (the joy, gratefulness, pleasure, and happiness of it) as if you have already attained it and are presently experiencing it. With your mind's eye see the pictures and hold it in front of your mind steadily and get it deep into your subconscious. Feel the feelings in your affirmations and visualizations: the stronger the feeling, the more powerful the affirmations effectiveness and the larger the chance it will come about. If your emotions strongly desire the end-result you are aiming for, each day will be a joy. You will be more than happy to do the things necessary to get there, no matter how hard they are. This is because you want the end goal stronger than you want to be comfortable in the moment.

> *"Imagination is everything. It is the preview of life's coming attractions."*
>
> Albert Einstein

Imagine you were in a video game and you could do whatever you want with no consequences. You could risk it all, you can do anything and not worry about failing or what people think about you. What would you do? Honestly, think about it: what would you do? Now, take a second and think about life like that. When you didn't have those barriers of fear preventing you from DOING, then you did DO. And that is why successful people are successful. That is why the visionaries lived out their visions of the future. They dared to do what others wouldn't even fathom. They think crazy and act crazy. You can sit around thinking of all kinds of creative ways to make money, but until you actually do them, they mean absolutely nothing—jack squat. You might as well have never of thought of them in the first place.

When you practice destiny affirmation, you are conjuring your dreams to reality. These dreams are no longer dreams. They are living, breathing actualities. They're alive! You won't believe it unless you see it, and you won't see it unless you believe it. You cannot allow room for doubt. Even if doubt enters your mind, that's okay, it's normal. Still, you must rebuke it and continue in faith. Consider James 1:6-7, "But when you ask, you must believe and not doubt, because the one who doubts is like a wave of the sea, blown and tossed by the wind. That person should not expect to receive anything from the Lord."

America boasts itself on individuality, but our school system still fails to promote it. If anything, our schools discourage it. We're so focused on learning facts, numbers and other inapplicable knowledge that won't actually help in the real world, that we lose our creativity. We grow up thinking we have to go to college to be a success or get some salary office job.

What happened to when you were 5-years-old, and you wanted to be an astronaut or the president? Well, you grew up and "reality set in." The world made it seem like you just couldn't beat the odds. You couldn't measure up. The chances of you being the 0.001% to achieve your dream were impossible, right? WRONG!

Screw 'em all! Where did they get those numbers anyway? "Someone told them." Who told them? God? No, I doubt that. If anything, God wants you to realize he created you for a purpose and that you are capable of achieving the dreams and desires he placed in your heart. For crying out loud, he gave you the tools to do it. You think God would create you, place dreams in you, make you unique, and give you talents and abilities for you to not be able to follow through? What kind of God is that? Not any God I know. Even if you don't believe in God. Do you think you happen to be on this earth for no apparent reason? Even if you were, you should make the most of it, and go all out. You only have one life. Don't waste it! Don't settle for average. Settle only for massive success—extraordinary accomplishment!

So, let's do a quick review. Our mind has two levels: a subconscious and a conscious. We think and act consciously (like your mind reading and processing these words to understand them or you trying to solve a problem) with our conscious mind. This is the level where we freely choose what we will.

The other, more mystical level is our subconscious mind. This is the level that holds our core beliefs and solves problems in a deeper way. We can influence our subconscious mind by actively and consciously choosing to suggest affirmations to it, whether negative or positive. The subconscious mind doesn't care if the suggestion is true or false in light of reality, it only believes what the conscious mind tells it. We can also influence our subconscious without even realizing it, which happens far too often than we would expect, which is why we must be careful to not dwell on negative thoughts or accept negative suggestions from ourselves or others. We must learn to recognize and subsequently thwart negative suggestions. Our subconscious mind then influences our conscious mind based on its accumulation of beliefs and values it has been programmed to believe, whether intentionally or not, by allowing us to either do or not do something. Therefore, by intentionally and consciously suggesting positively-affirming beliefs to our subconscious mind on purpose, we can program it to have a set of beliefs that are congruent with our destiny. We can then begin to work out our destiny as our conscious minds are influenced, motivated, and compelled by our subconscious to create plans, set goals, and take the necessary actions that will get us to where we want to be.

"In the beginning, there will be conflict between where you are or what you have, and what you are accepting subconsciously. One of the primary functions of the subconscious, however, is to resolve conflicts between what we are thinking about and what we are experiencing in our reality, and because our subconscious is creative, it will begin to create what we are thinking about and what we are visualizing."

Dr. Robert Anthony

CHAPTER 3
GOALS!

"If you want to be happy, set a goal that commands your thoughts, liberates your energy, and inspires your hopes."

Andrew Carnegie

The Importance of Goals

To be successful, you must set goals. Period. You cannot be successful without goals. It's simply not possible. The mind doesn't reach toward achievement until it has clearly defined objectives. Your GPS doesn't give you a route unless you put in an address. In the same way, you as a human being, will not give yourself a way to reach the desired target if there is no target clearly defined. When you set a goal, your mind is compelled to find a route and begins moving in that direction until you receive the "You've arrived at your destination!" notification. Aspirations, wants, and desires that are not clearly defined and that are not followed by actions are mere wishes. You might as well have never hoped or wanted those wishes because they were a waste of time.

It requires a powerful emotional drive to conjure your mental picture of how you want your life to look like from abstract to reality. You must want it, like, really want it. You have to have a strong, all-encompassing desire. When you have a chief, central desire and put it in the form of a written, measurable goal, then the motivating force behind your desire propels you into action. You not only act at high levels, but you love doing so. That's what's so magical about setting your objectives in an area you are passionate about. When you want to do something, love doing it, or simply want to achieve a goal very badly, your subconscious mind starts working overtime to produce effective plans and ideas. Your emotions, when under the control of your mind, can be funneled into your will. You then willingly take effective action and do it out of joy, not merely out of necessity.

How to Set Goals

Setting goals is far simpler than people make it out to be. You want to take time to really think, pray, and meditate about how you want your life to be. You should set financial, professional, personal, health, emotional, spiritual, and relational goals. You don't have to set goals in all these areas, but it is a good idea to do so. You don't want to neglect one area of your life, or else you may compensate for one area with over focus in another and then come years later to realize how much of a wreck the neglected area in your life has become. Balance is both wise and healthy. Balance does good to your body, soul, and mind. You should appropriately tend to the various aspects of each of those three realms of yourself.

First, you should gain a clear understanding of your values. Your values influence, sustain and maintain your beliefs. Values are the foundation of your beliefs. You should take the time to write down what you value most in life. Values are the why to your purpose. These are your innermost convictions—your heart's desires. These are determined by your subconscious. (Remember, you can influence your subconscious and what it believes by consciously deciding what should be through destiny affirmations.) Values are what you really stand for and believe in.

Once you have established what you perceive to be your values, you should also assess your beliefs. We've already gone over this, but it's necessary to understand to establish effective goals. If you are ignorant of your values and beliefs, you will look back 5 to 10 years from now and realize you've wasted time working towards the objective that didn't really matter to you. "Suppose one of you wants to build a tower. Won't you first sit down and estimate the cost to see if you have enough money to complete it? For if you lay, the foundation and are not able to finish it, everyone who sees it will ridicule you, saying, 'This person began to build and wasn't able to finish.' Or suppose a king is about to go to war against another king. Won't he first sit down and consider whether he is able with ten thousand men to oppose the one coming against him with twenty thousand?" (Luke 14:28-31) If you have a big, nearly impossible goal you want to attain, you should also have the accompanying beliefs to support it.

Your mindset is your money. Your mind is your employee, your value system is your army, and your beliefs are your troops. If you have limited or shaky beliefs, you won't be able to attain what you want because you don't believe you really can. You, therefore, won't be able to defeat your competition, and you won't be able to slay your giants. If David hadn't gone into battle with the conviction that with the help of his God and with the trust in his own abilities that he could defeat Goliath, he would have never killed Goliath. But David believed firmly. David understood the power of belief and trusted in his potential. The size of the goals you accomplish is only in proportion to the size you believe in your potential to be. You have unlimited capacity, but you get to choose how much of what you believe. Be like David and choose unlimited potential. No giant in your life can defeat you. You are unstoppable!

"You become as small as your controlling desire; as great as your dominant aspiration."

James Allen

Now think of the top five to ten goals you can think of. I mean big goals. The top five to ten you want to accomplish in the next year, five years or ten years. These can even be life goals, it doesn't matter. These should be the ones you desire the most. You should write them in the first-person, present tense. For example, "I have a $10 million net-worth by 2023," or "I am doubling my income annually." I want you to make it a habit of writing these goals down every day, preferably in the morning. It's also a good idea to write these at night as well. This gets you focused on your main goals and keeps them in the forefront of your mind like destiny affirmations. You are informing your subconscious of the direction you are going.

Set BIG Goals

Think BIG! You cannot afford to think any smaller. If you think small, then you will settle for less than you're capable of. Look at life as if there is a solution to any problem and that there is no limitation to accomplishing anything. All things are possible. Now that you took that into consideration: what would you do? Okay, does what you just thought of when I asked that compare with the goals you came up with earlier? Are your previous goals smaller? You should choose the bigger, loftier goal. Could your goal be too aspirational? When is a goal too big or too ridiculous? Never! The unattainable and seemingly impossible goals are the ones I've been trying to get you to desire and write down.

"When a man has put a limit on what he will do, he has put a limit on what he can do."

Charles M. Schwab

Prioritize goals

You want to set your goals in order of importance. The ones you want to achieve the most should be higher up in priority. This is especially important for monthly, weekly, and daily goals. I keep a phone app that lists my weekly and daily goals in list form. I prioritize them with a system that works for me. I would like to explain a system of prioritization I learned a couple years back. In this system, you rate your goals in the level of importance from A to E. A being the most important—something that must be done today. E being the least important—something that doesn't really affect my day or future if I don't do it right now. Within these alphabetical levels are other levels: 1-3. For example, if I had three A tasks for the day, I can list them in chronological order of which ones I should do first. One can be A1, the other A2, and the final A3.

Chunk n' Dunk

You've probably heard this question asked: "How do you eat an elephant?" If you haven't, then the answer is one bite at a time. You must break goals into smaller goals and sub-goals (or tasks and sub-tasks). You can have a big goal and the mindset to back it up, but if you don't separate and organize it into smaller chunks, you will become overwhelmed—you wouldn't be able to swallow it! You have to break your goal into smaller chunks and then dunk 'em (complete them)! The more organized and smaller the chunkin', the easier the dunkin'! And once you get on a win-streak of dunkin', no one will be able to stop you. You will be on fire and your constant wins, in completing your tasks, moving you closer and closer to your desired goal will cause a snowball effect that will have you energized and laser focused! The secret of getting ahead is getting started.

> *"The secret of getting started is breaking your complex, overwhelming tasks into small manageable tasks, then starting on the first one."*
>
> Mark Twain

Deadlines

For each goal and subgoal, you must set deadlines. Setting a deadline is like making a promise to yourself. Now that your conscious has made a pact with your subconscious to complete a specific task on time, your subconscious will keep you consciously accountable. Without deadlines that you set a high priority on (meaning you have a conviction of completing on time), then you will not complete goals on time or maybe not at all. You will continue to procrastinate and put them off. You cannot compromise on deadlines. You must promise yourself you will meet the deadline and keep yourself accountable. If you give yourself a break, you will procrastinate forever and never get anything significant accomplished in life. Setting a deadline and taking it seriously will allow you to be massively successful in every goal you set.

Reviewing and Assessing Goals

You want to constantly assess the many areas of life for which you have set goals. You want to see how far along you have come.

Compare yourself only to yourself. Don't compare your goals to someone else's goals or achievements. Be true to yourself and your values. Also, don't let anyone tell you your goals are wrong or selfish. It's always wise to take negative feedback and look at it in an objective manner, but you cannot let it control you. You cannot allow yourself to be swayed by the opinions and mindsets of others. Most people spend their entire lives giving their opinions about things they know little about and have no good reason to do so. Someone may tell you that your idea is too big or ridiculous. Has that person ever achieved great success? No? Then, don't give them the time of day. Other people have influenced you your whole life and programmed you with the type of thinking of the poor and middle-class that we've spent the past two chapters getting rid of. Don't let them come back with doubt. You should consider feedback. Feedback is good because you could be wrong, you always could be wrong. But you must make your own choices. Don't ever listen to someone else's advice out of ignorance or fear, especially when they don't know what they're talking about.

Remember how I talked about David and Goliath earlier? Well, everyone thought David was crazy about taking on Goliath and didn't think he could defeat him. David was just a little shepherd boy who had never trained for or had ever experienced combat. Goliath, however, has trained for battle since he was a boy. Besides, he was a giant! He was the Philistine's champion. David didn't let what anyone else thought about him, or his potential throw him off from his purpose. He stayed true to himself and his destiny and did what he believed what he could do. If David would have let the opinions of others, even his own brothers, affect him, he would have hesitated and failed. But David didn't give in to fear or doubt. He was laser focused and understood the power of belief, who he was, and his destiny. David also remembered smaller victories, like defeating a bear and a lion. That's another reason it is important to break down your goals into smaller goals and sub-goals. Past victories support future ventures and supply you with confidence and faith in your next battle.

"Whatever the mind of man can conceive and believe, it can achieve."

Napoleon Hill

CHAPTER 4
CREATE A PLAN

Why a Plan?

You don't form a masterpiece on a whim. You first form a picture of it in your mind, and then you begin the process of sculpting or painting. You don't have every detail, but you know the base form you're going for. Your life is your masterpiece. You should take the time and write out a solid, yet flexible plan for your success. The process, however, is progressive and shifts, changes, and evolves to fit your best interest as you yourself progress and evolve as an individual. Still, that calls for a plan. Wishes and dreams without a plan are only wishes and dreams without a plan: they won't actually get you anywhere.

> *"You create your own future as you go along."*
>
> Winston Churchill

Creativity On Command

Big goals and set-in-stone deadlines force the creativity to achieve your goals. By committing to accomplishing a goal and setting a deadline, your mind is forced to expand beyond its everyday capacity and is opened to receive from the infinite creative source from above. Our brains adrenalize and rise far beyond the amount of energy it uses on a day-to-day basis and then, quite literally, kicks itself outside the box of conventional thinking and compels you to think up creative ideas that you would have never really thought of before setting such a lofty goal and/or deadline. What's happening is: your mind is no longer going about life on autopilot, and instead is tapping into a creative force that is outside of itself.

When you set goals and you are inspired with all sorts of creative ideas that begin to form into an actual plan, and you write out that plan, and it becomes a life or business model, your mind becomes joyously overwhelmed as this euphoric feeling rushes through your being. It's like this crazy, addictive drug that's really good for you. You feel so alive because your destiny is being worked out before your eyes. It's insane when you see your dream go to a goal to a plan, and then you begin executing the plan and reaping the results. This is the success principles of the universe in action. You may be thinking, "What's all this spiritual stuff have to do with becoming a millionaire?" A lot! Ask a millionaire. They'll tell you the same thing. (Remember, what I said about balance earlier? How do you expect long-term success in your soul and body when your spirit is a mess?) Your spirit is so big it fills the whole room. That's why when somebody walks in a room, they can either light it up or dull it down. We are energy at our core. Not only is our spirit energy, but our body is, too. Everything in the universe is energy. Energy can neither be created nor destroyed. And don't you remember what Einstein's $E=mc2$ was all about? (That's too much to get into for the focus of this subject matter.)

You have to think outside the box—don't be conventional. How can you use your unique talents and passions to create something that generates wealth? You must push your creative boundaries. You are far more creative than you realize. The problem most of us have is that we have been conditioned through school, rule-following, and other means that have ultimately suppressed our creativity. Your creative muscle is still there, you've just stopped working it out. Our schooling systems and their outdated methods have gone at length to establish practices that destroy the creative capacities of children. Life has pressured you into something you don't have to be. It may work for some people, but not everyone was created for the 9-to-5 cubical life. The "real world" and all it's (false) pictures of the average American life has shoved down your throat the "this is what you should do to live a 'successful' life" mentality. When you were a kid, you were super creative, remember? What happened? Well, you just stopped using the creative parts of your brain and switched over to the other, more analytical and fact-focused parts. To quote Brian Chesky, CEO and co-founder of Airbnb: "Growing up you're taught to look straight ahead; you don't get rewarded for being disruptive, you just go to the principal's office, and I was there quite often." (Me, too!)

You can open and improve the creative side of your brain. It simply takes effort and practice. Your creative abilities are like a muscle: they will be strong and toned when used consistently, and they will become weak and shrink when used little or not at all. The only way to grow your muscles is by overextending their capabilities until they rip. They then heal and grow back stronger due to muscular adaptation. If you go to the gym and do the same amount of reps, sets, and weight, and never increase the weight, then your muscles will never grow any stronger. Your muscles will only be at the same level, in neutral, and since time is moving forward, even if you're in neutral, you're actually moving backward because you could be improving, but you chose not to—you're settling for less or average. By continually stretching your creative boundaries, you are forcing your creative abilities to go outside of their normal capacity causing them to rip, adapt, and evolve to be able to keep up with the increased load that has been forced upon them.

Your job is to figure out the what and the action. It is your subconscious mind's job to give you the how. Then you can do the how until you get the what.

Always Add Value

The first self-help book I read was How to Win Friends and Influence People by Dale Carnegie, and it completely revolutionized and flipped my thinking about so much in my life. It showed me that most everything in life was all about other people and adding value to them. That was the book that turned me onto the pursuit of the development and growth of myself and got me interested in business and entrepreneurship.

Your plan should have some place it adds values to others—to your customers. This should be a key element to your plan, probably the backbone or mission statement. To be successful in any business venture, you have to acquire the Value Adding Mindset. All millionaires have this mindset and know how to use it. The Value-Adding Mindset understands that for you to reap value, you must sow value and lots of it! I spoke to a mentor of mine recently, who happens to be a very successful multimillionaire, and he said, "You can add value anywhere." You must find a need and fill it. You should always give the customer more in useful value than the customer pays in monetary value. In the end, that's really what business and economics are all about, right? Exchanging value!

Here's a quick overview of how you can add value: You must first choose a niche (or target market). Then, you must identify the problems and shortcomings your target market is facing. Finally, you should then find, create, and provide a solution to their problem(s). Boom! That is adding value. You want to identify the missing piece to their puzzle and become that piece. If you can successfully offer people value, they will literally give you whatever price you ask for in exchange.

People only pay for something that is useful—that helps solve a problem in their lives. You should think in terms of what do people want? What do people want that they are willing to pay for? What problems do people have that I can develop and offer a solution to? This can be either a product or a service, but it first starts out as an idea. An idea of a solution to a problem.

Mastermind Group

All the super successful of the world have had, what Napoleon Hill coined, a Mastermind Group. You must get together with people who are smarter and more creative than you. This is the equivalent to a board of directors of a corporation. Within a Mastermind Group, you are able to access the resources, creativity, and expertise of others that have different skillsets and storehouses of knowledge than you. The mastermind should have a chief aim and purpose that everyone supports, and members should have similar values. It's important for you to choose a group of people consisting of the different domains of expertise that will help you and the group in the attainment of your agreed upon purpose and objectives. You should acquire people who agree with and support the mission of your goals or the goals of your company, but who also come from various areas of study and background.

If you don't have time to create a Mastermind Group, at least make it a major goal to seek out mentors. You'll be surprised how willing other successful people are willing to teach and mentor you. If a prospective mentor is in the same business you want to go in, you may be thinking "Why would they want more competition?" or "Why would they give me the time of day?" Forget those thoughts. They are doubts that mean nothing. Go and ask. You have nothing to lose anyway. The worse they could say is no.

> *"Though one may be overpowered, two can defend themselves. A cord of three strands is not quickly broken."*
>
> Ecclesiastes 4:12

Other Thoughts On Creating a Plan

Find a way for money to work for you, not the other way around; or find a way to get other people to work for you, not you work for other people. How do you do that? Well, investing! In what? Stock market, bonds, and real estate? Well, yes, but also (more importantly) through ideas, products, and services. This is wealth-generation, not making money. Money is already made, now the job is to get the money to you. Your plans should get people to give you money. That's probably the biggest difference between the rich and the poor! Yes, they work, and they've worked hard for what they've amassed. But even more important than working hard is that they've worked smarter, and thus have reaped the rewards in store for those who work smarter. (Chapter Six is entirely focused on investing.)

A very powerful habit I encourage to learn is that of planning out your day the night before. This is a habit of many successful people. Doing this allows your subconscious mind to work on the tasks all night long and creatively solve problems for the day to come. You will be more ready and more creative for the day, and it will allow you more time in the morning to exercise, pray, or meditate.

You have to be laser-focused, aware of your time management and constantly assess and take note of what works and doesn't work. This is how you evolve, and it takes time. There is no shortcut to success. The super successful give 1000% effort. No, that was not a typo. That was one thousand percent. Not 100%, not 110%, but 1000%. Most people work at 20-80% effort. 100% won't cut it and neither will just a little over the top at 110%. The only way to achieve massive success is 1000%.

CHAPTER 5
YOUR GREATEST ASSET

Time!

Show me your schedule, and I'll show you your priorities. You use your time on what's important to you. If doing nothing and being lazy is important to you, then you will spend a lot of time procrastinating and getting nowhere in life. Then, when you're older and regret all your wasted years, you'll spend the majority of your time complaining and using excuses to try to justify why you're entitled to everything and how much everything is against you and everything is everyone else's fault, including your circumstances. This is the victim mentality (more about that in the Self-discipline chapter).

What's one of the number one excuse people use for not doing something? "I don't have enough time." Umm... yes, you do! Warren Buffet, Brian Chesky, Elon Musk, Mark Zuckerberg, Donald Trump, Lebron James, and Jeff Bezos all have the same amount of time in the day as you do. The only difference of time between them and you are that they use their time wisely. They understand the importance of time: time is money. And if you believe that too, then you should track, calculate, manage, and invest time just as you do your money. Don't ever say you don't have enough time. That is a lie. Don't lie to yourself or anyone else. Own up to your responsibility for time and become massively accountable to yourself on how you steward it.

Time Stewardship

Why do you waste time? I don't know, but you do not have time to waste time. It's all you have! Well, at least it was all you've been freely given. You only have so much time, and the longer you wait and don't act, you are throwing away precious potential and maybe even world-changing inventions, breakthroughs, and ideas that can be solutions to major world problems. Out of everything you have in life, time is what you're given freely (along with talents and ability). You have a duty to steward it. You must adopt a hatred for wasting time. If it doesn't provide any value to you, your life values, or anyone else, then it should not be a priority. It should not be on your schedule.

Where do you want to be in five years? Okay. Where are you now? Sure. Why are you still here? Why are you not there, yet? I'm sure there's plenty of reasons (excuses!), but I'm sure one of the major reasons is because you're not maximizing your time. Do you still watch those three hours of Netflix a night? Do you catch an extra hour of scrolling through Instagram instead of an extra couple chapters of a book? Still playing (addicted to) that video games? You must identify the time you are wasting and really consider if that time could be better used by investing it in yourself and your future. If you have committed to too many events and opportunities, you need to learn to say no.

Can you have massive action and balance, or must one be sacrificed for the other? Are you really limitless and have unlimited capacity? That's for you to decide. You can have both, but it's a matter of priority. Energy has no shortage. Still, you must work smarter not harder. Become smarter by inventorying and using your time smarter. Learn what gives you the most leverage—the most value—and do that more. Remember: this isn't just for you; it's for your family, your legacy, your customers, your employees, and everyone that you will have an impact on in life.

Patience

Disclaimer: I'm not saying everything comes quick. You must learn patience. Unless you create the next Apple, Google or Amazon, you won't become a bazillionaire overnight. And even all those companies had to learn and sow hordes of patience, perseverance, and hard work before ever reaping the profits. Do not be deceived, get rich quick schemes DO NOT work. Every farmer knows that you don't plant a seed and come to it the next day and ask, "Where's the harvest?!"

CHAPTER 6
DON'T WORK FOR MONEY

You probably grew up hearing from your parents, your professor, your best friend or whoever, to not spend all your money and to set aside a portion of it in a saving's account each time you get paid. The rich know that saving doesn't do anything. Saving actually makes you poorer. You must invest! Saving is a habit of the poor and middle class. The poor and middle class spend their entire lives working hard. Then, they either desperately save their money to "protect it," or they spend all their hard-earned money on nothing of any real, lasting, or beneficial value.

Investing Trumps Saving

Don't work for money. Make money work for you! The rich understand this more than any other class. You reap what you sow. This concept was the cornerstone of The Richest Man in Babylon: "each piece of gold is a little worker to make more gold." Each of your dollars is a worker of yours to make more dollars. You can either fire him and exchange him for something else (like a Starbucks' coffee, an expensive meal, or designer clothing), you can hide and bury him in the ground where he will do nothing at all but lose value, or you can employ him and put him to work. If you want to be rich, you better put him to work. Investing trumps saving every time!

You literally cannot afford to sit passively and just save enough to get by in case of emergency. In reality, you're actually losing money by leaving it in a bank account. The average annual rate of inflation is 3.22%. No bank's savings accounts' rates are higher than that. You're better off having your money in an S&P 500 index fund (which is recommended by Warren Buffet as your best investment choice). The average annualized total return for the S&P 500 index over the past 90 years is 9.8 percent (much better than a bank's 1.7%). Yeah, it sounds risky but if the market crashes, just ride it out. The market always rises again and higher than before. Besides, it has to keep up with inflation either way, and safe mutual funds give on average more than 5%. So, you're at least not losing money and are actually making a pretty significant (not extravagant—but significant) amount on your money you aren't spending or using. If you aren't spending it, at least invest it into investment vehicles.

The Power of Owning vs. Working

Did you know that 85% of millionaires were "self-made" and didn't work a typical 9-5 job? When you work hard at a job, you only reap the rate you agreed to work for. You can only work so many hours. You can only make so much money. If you're salary, that annual amount is the most you will make for the year.

Building wealth, for the most part, always involves owning multiple streams of income, such as businesses, side-projects, royalties, stocks, bonds, notes, any passive sources of income, and other forms of investment. If you're working a salary 9-5 job, you could be spending your extra time creating new streams of income. You should not be reliant on only one stream! What if you lose your job tomorrow? What will you fall back on? The idea is to continue to create enough streams to the point where you don't even have to work anymore. This is passive income. This is your money working for you to make you more money. I suggest you never move from a stream if it gives you steady income (unless it's too much of a hassle for too little income). Even if you work a full-time job and your other streams are equal or greater in wealth-generation than your full-time job, you can use your full-time job to invest in current or new streams. At this point, you're multiplying streams with existing streams. This is how companies like Amazon and Google grow at exponential rates, they use their profits as investments back into themselves.

The most powerful investments are investing in ideas, products, and services. These investments produce massive ROI's. This is wealth-generation, not making money. Money is already made, now the job is to get the money to you. Your investments should get people to give you money. If it's investment in starting a company, it should get money to you. As a business owner, you retain profits, not paychecks.

The majority of the rich have used real estate as a vehicle for wealth. Andrew Carnegie, the wealthiest man in America during the early 20th Century, once said, "Ninety percent of all millionaires become so through owning real estate." He went on to say, "More money has been made in real estate than in all industrial investments combined" and, "The wise young man or wage earner of today invests his money in real estate." John D. Rockefeller, the richest man to ever live, made his first fruits in the oil industry and expanded his empire to include immense amounts of real estate because he understood the value of real estate as an investment tool. Real estate always appreciates, and you can make money right when you buy it.

Survive to Thrive

You should only save money that you plan to invest in a future venture. I make it a habit to only keep so much money in an easily accessible checking's account and my other money in savings accounts and highly liquid ETFs. I discipline myself to refuse from spending anything other than what's in my main checking account. This causes me to stay frugal and have healthy spending habits. This motivates me to control my spending and motivates me to work smarter—forcing me to come up with more creative ideas to try and dominate. Like I've reiterated time and time again is that success is a choice. Failure is a choice. Poverty is a choice. Wealth is a choice. Becoming a millionaire is a choice. Where you are now is a result of your choices. Where you will be in the future is determined solely by your choices. Your choices are determined by the way you think—your thoughts—your mindset! What determines whether you are rich, or poor is your spending habits. There are rich and poor spending habits. What you do right now with your money reflects your spending habits. Habits are determined by the neurological patterns within your brain—your mindset! If you want to be a millionaire, then assume a Millionaire Mindset Now!

Give Now!

Giving is investing. Rich people are generous people. Have you ever wondered why the world's richest people are also the world's biggest philanthropists? "Ah!" you might say, "but that's because they have so much money, they can afford to give." Well, not necessarily so. The rich understand money better than most. They understand the point of money isn't to possess it but to dispense of it. Then, lo and behold, they have more money than they can spend. So why hold onto it anyway? Most people may find this concept very hard to believe, but that's because they hold onto their money so tightly and desperately that their hands are never opening to receive any more money. No wonder the universe doesn't give them money. They're so obsessed with themselves and their own wants and needs and fail to see the bigger picture. Greed eats up people and tears them apart. You have to learn to let go and give out of a generous heart. This is faith in action, and you are rewarded for it, trust me. I believe largely in tithes and offerings, and I always pay them first, not last. And no wonder I always seem to have more than before. It's a strange and paradoxical concept, but it is real. Remember: you reap what you sow!

CHAPTER 7
SELF-DISCIPLINE

This is an absolute, no questions asked, 100% MUST to becoming successful. There is no success without self-discipline. There is no leadership without self-discipline. There are no results without self-discipline (besides the negative results you probably really don't want). I'm not only referring to self-discipline concerning money, but I'm referring to every area of life: financial, emotional, spiritual, physical health, and so on. You must master your emotions. Mastering your emotions is probably the most important self-discipline to learn. If you let your emotions drive you, they will determine what you do, how you do it, when you do it, why you do it, for how long you do it, or why not do it at all in the first place.

Living an emotionally-driven life will destroy you and your future, and this will squander all your potential. "But I don't wanna," well, quite frankly it doesn't matter if you wanna or not cus' you gotta! You must, or you will not achieve your goals and objectives. You will not live the life you want.

Discipline is doing what you really don't want to do now, so you can do the things you really want to later. It feels somewhat of a sacrifice, but it is simply sowing the seeds necessary to reap the harvest you want.

Responsibility

You must take full responsibility for everything you do, and that is done to you. Because how you think gets you to where you are, you are therefore responsible whether you acknowledge it or not. So, the sooner you take 100% responsibility for everything that either happens to you or because of you, the sooner you can start to progress and create the life you want.

It's easy to take responsibility for things that happen because of us, but it tends to be harder for us to take responsibility for when things happen to us. But remember, what we dwell on with our minds is attracted to it, whether good or bad. This happens since our subconscious mind doesn't know the difference between what is factual or not, only what the conscious mind tells it is right. When we fill our minds with negative assumptions like worrying thoughts such as, "I'm going to fail this test," or "I'm a failure," our subconscious mind receives that information from the conscious mind as fact and says to itself, "Okay, that must be what I want." The subconscious mind then begins working out plans and working behind the scenes, putting together situations, and taking opportunities that would lead you to attaining what "you want."

So, if you're subconscious mind thinks "I will always be poor," then it will figure out a way to always be poor, or if it thinks "I cannot do _____, that's impossible; I will always be _____," then it will make sure that which you believe on the inside becomes what is true on the outside. Therefore, what happens "*to you*" is actually the same thing as what happens *because of you*. There is no difference between the two besides our conditioned understanding of the two. Thus, we need to remove the lines between the two and accept that we are totally and utterly responsible for everything that happens to us. We are 100% responsible for every aspect of our lives. Whatever happens or doesn't happen to you—either what you want or don't want—is a direct result of your thinking, actions, or inaction.

You create the life you live, and no one else. If we continue to believe we have no responsibility for things that happen "to us," we will continue to look to outside forces to blame. When we don't take responsibility for something, we give up control of that thing. When we blame others, we give up control. When we blame others, we lie and deceive ourselves. Why do we lie to ourselves? Because it's easier and it feels good for us to release responsibility over something because we don't have to worry or think about it. But you cannot create the future you desire if you keep on lying and taking shortcuts. You will continue to go backward. If you want to go backward and not forward, then go ahead and blame everyone and everything else for things that happen to you.

There is no good in blaming and complaining. These are negative grumblings that destroy your inner power. You become less and less disciplined as a result, and therefore become less and less powerful. Releasing responsibility releases power. When you take responsibility for something, you are therefore responsible for it. You take hold and can control it. You can literally change the circumstances and situations around you to fit what best fits your perception of how your life and the world around you should be. But to do so, you must take full responsibility for everything in your life.

Motivation

The key to self-discipline is motivation. You have to want the larger reward of achieving a long-term goal more than the smaller, usually more temporal and fleeting, "reward" or experience of a short-term indulgence. This goes back to your purpose and destiny. If the achievement of your goal of becoming a millionaire by a certain deadline is more valuable than short-term pleasure, then you won't pull out your investment or savings early, you won't go in debt for that new car, and you won't buy that new product that came out. "But, oh! They seem so attractive and pretty, and besides, it'll make me look good and feel good. Doesn't feeling rich motivate me to want to become rich more?" WRONG! Those are all excuses. Don't give into your ancient, physiological reward system.

Don't try to live a lifestyle you can't afford. Trust me, it's not worth it. Trying to keep up with the Joneses is a social-economic trap. You don't want to keep up with the Joneses. Who the hell are they anyway? You want to crush the Joneses! You want everybody trying to keep up with you. Screw what anyone has to say about it. You'll be far more successful than they will, and it will show with time. You reap what you sow, don't be deceived! Spending money on expensive and useless things keep you in the poor and middle-class brackets. You don't need those things! That's what poor people do—they save money for it to go to waste or spend money on things that have no real or lasting value. The feeling you get for owning that doo-dad is not worth losing money over. Those things depreciate in value the moment you buy them. Don't fall for the psychological trap. It's just chemicals—endorphins—rushing through your brain telling you "Hey! That thing will make you feel so good!" Yeah, and you buy it, and it does exactly what your mind was telling you. It makes you feel great, right? And then, boom! The feeling goes away and honestly, you probably feel worse than you did before because you just threw away some of your little money workers that can be making you more money. You have less financial security and now more stress; especially if you go into debt to get it! It's not healthy at all.

So, screw the Jones'! They're the ones creating the social-psychological keep-up game and selling you the things they're promoting. They're the smart ones. They're profiting off of you and laughing to the bank. You can overcome them. You can beat them. Just say no. That's it; nothing more. Just say, "NO." There is no pressure to say yes. Say no. Don't do it. You can say no, and you will. You know how I know that? Because I know you are destined for success, right? You do believe that, don't you? Good. Now get out there and live your life how you want to: happy, wealthy and successful!

Leadership

Your level of leadership is determined by your ability to influence. Influence is gained by casting a vision that people willingly follow. The best leaders cast a vision that empowers, energizes and fills people with enthusiasm to work towards that common vision in a powerful effort of synergy. Leadership takes intentionality. How can you be expected to lead anyone if you cannot even lead yourself? The most excellent and renowned leaders are even greater leaders of themselves and their lives. Leadership is a skill necessary for success and is a discipline that must be learned. (Yes, leadership can be learned!)

Learning Never Stops at Graduation

You might be graduated from high school or college, but every successful person has taken a life course in constant learning. Top CEOs in the world are averaged at reading 60 or more books per year. That's about 5 books a month! I don't care if you're "not a reader," you better become one now and do it quickly! I was never a reader, I hated reading assigned literature in high school. But when my mind was opened to the fact that to become a success—a really big success, when I realized my purpose and destiny—I got right on it. Last year I set a goal to read in March to read 40 books by the end of the year. Guess how many I read by the end of December? Eighty! That's right, 80 books! I accomplished double my goal. That's pretty good for someone who used to hate reading.

Believe me, once you determine to read X number of books and you actually start reading them and knocking them out quicker and quicker; and you actually start seeing the results manifest (like your income doubling or tripling or seeing your productivity levels and efficiency skyrocket)—you will only want to read more and more. It becomes an addiction. You no longer dread reading, but you love it. You can't wait to go home and get filled up with some life-changing knowledge instead of watching TV and "taking it easy." You have to feed your mind. Money doesn't come to the passive, it comes to the active. Money comes to those who continually invest in themselves and their minds.

However, you don't want to stop at just books. You want to listen to podcasts, take online courses, and attend conferences. There are countless free or at least relatively cheap resources out there scattered around the internet. You can get most of it with as little as a simple Google search. I would say the three top most important skills you should learn to be successful as a businessperson is sales (which includes marketing, persuasion, influence, and charisma—yes charisma can be learned), investment, and management (or leadership). Especially focus on hard and soft skills needed for your specific industry.

CHAPTER 8
ENEMIES OF SUCCESS

I'd like to use this chapter to highlight and overview some of the enemies of success. These are the enemies of your future and destiny and should be treated as such. You should take every action necessary to prevent and fight these enemies of success. These enemies seem like they are allies because they bring you a feeling of comfort. Comfort itself is an enemy of success. You will never become successful if you live your life and make decisions based on the comfort they give you. To reap large rewards, you must sow large risk: this is not comfortable. The more uncomfortable you feel should be an indicator of the level of success it can bring you. This uncomfortableness comes in many forms such as fear and doubt. You must be aware of these feelings. Feelings, when untamed, are your enemies. Feelings, when intentionally channeled, are your allies. If you correctly target your emotions appropriately, they will be powerful tools in achieving your goals and creating the type of life you want to live.

Excuses and Procrastination

You must take full responsibility for everything you do, and that is done to you. I mean extreme responsibility! If you aren't happy about how your life is at the moment, then do something about it. If you blame everything and everyone else but yourself for your circumstances or how you feel, then you will keep searching outside yourself for solutions. No one else is the problem, and no one else has the solution. You are both the problem (because of your problematic thinking, not you as a person) and the solution. By that I mean you are responsible. And the sooner you accept that, the sooner you can fix it and stop complaining and blaming everyone else. Complaining doesn't do anything but breed more negativity, sinking you in deeper trouble. Push through. You have to get over it. You're the master of your emotions. Control them! Don't let them control you. Happiness is a choice. Depression is a choice. Desire is a choice. Anger is a choice. You have been divinely bestowed with free will.

You have the power within you to *choose* how you feel. If you do not believe you are the master of your thoughts, emotions, and actions, then you will think you are not responsible for everything that you do and that happens to you. If you think you are not responsible for everything that you do and that happens to you, then you are calling yourself powerless. *If you think you are powerless, you will be powerless* to change your circumstances and will continue to be a victim. You will continue to be a drifter instead of a steerer of your life ship. Stop being a victim and stop living a lie. You have the creative power to change and shift your circumstances. You can get what you want. You must take massive, total, and complete responsibility for everything that you do (and don't do) and that is done to you.

When we don't take responsibility for the way things are in our lives, we fall victim to (no pun intended) the Victim Mentality. The Victim Mentality is the reverse of the Millionaire Mindset. It is the exact opposite of how millionaires think. The Victim Mentality basically blames everyone and everything else for their current circumstances. There is no one to blame besides you (because of your erroneous thinking—you may have had negative or false thoughts concerning something, it could be a number of reasons, but the root goes back to you and the way you think). Everything in your life, from the amount of money you make to your health is a direct result (effect) of you (the cause). When you assume the

Victim Mentality, you forsake the Millionaire Mindset and give up your power to change and create what you desire. Don't let anything or anyone master you—not circumstances, not your mind or logic, not your feelings—let only you (the REAL YOU) control you and your destiny.

> *"It's easier to go from failure to success than it is from excuses to success."*
>
> John C. Maxwell

Fear and Failure

When you set a goal, considerations (abstract limitations or all the reasons "you cannot") and roadblocks (concrete obstacles) flood your brain. These were already in your subconscious but have only now been brought to your awareness. The more specific, and measurable the goal(s), the more considerations and roadblocks may come to your mind. This should be expected. **If any goal is worth pursuing, it should come with a myriad of fears and doubts.**

"It is impossible to live without failing at something, unless you live so cautiously that you might as well not have lived at all, in which case you have failed by default."

J. K. Rowling

When asked about the major problem facing the United States during the Great Depression, President Roosevelt replied, "It is not a question of majors and minors; we have, but one problem and that is to stop fear and supplant it with faith." The way to fight and ward off fear is to replace it with faith, or courage. Henry Ford didn't let the great economic collapse of the Great Depression deter him from his goals. He continued, with courage, to persist with laser-like focus and determination to bring his dream (of creating an automobile that every American could afford) to reality because he had the Millionaire Mindset. He was driven by his dream and set goals to achieve it. Though all the forces of the Universe seemed to be against him, he was energized by the strong desire to accomplish his goals and dreams, which thus inspired him with creativity to work those goals and dreams into plans with practical action-steps. This creativity birthed the assembly line, which in turn radically changed production and manufacturing forever.

Fear comes in many forms. There is the fear of failure, fear of loss, fear of being ostracized, fear of death, fear of looking stupid, fear of living alone, fear of public speaking, fear of what others may think, and on and on and on. You may fear quitting your job because you don't want to fail at pursuing your passion and opening that business you've always wanted to run. You may fear investing in that startup because you may lose all your savings. You may fear asking that girl out because she may so no or even worse. The good news is fear doesn't really exist. Fear is only part of the imagination of the human mind. It is not real. Fear is a liar, because fear is a lie.

"For God has not given us a spirit of fear and timidity, but of power, love, and self-discipline."

2 Timothy 1:7

Fear is not real, but it feels very real, especially when you face failure. When you fail, your mind is bombarded with fear and doubt. You start to doubt your abilities and destiny. But there's one thing about failure that the rich and successful know: FAILURE MAXIMIZES SUCCESS! Your mindset of failure is as equally important as your mindset concerning success. This is because they are complementary to one another. They are one in the same. What do I mean by that? *How you handle failure determines your level of success.* Successful people see failures as learning experiences. This motivates them to get back up and keep going until they succeed. The world's most successful have had far many more failures than they have had successes. They succeeded because they didn't take failure as an answer. This is because they knew success is their destiny. It's yours, too, if you'd only except it! You must put on the Winner Mindset. I plan to write an entire book solely on the subject of fear itself. I believe fear is the greatest repellant to success.

> *"No man ever became great or good except through many and great mistakes."*
>
> William E. Gladstone

The Positive and Negative Powers of Normalization

We adapt to the future and change quicker than we realize. This is called normalization, or adaptation. This is good because we become used to higher levels of learning and experience and can, therefore, grow at exponential and highly efficient rates. For example, some people are used to generating millions, even billions, of dollars because that is normal to them (my prayers and hope is that you would get to that point!) They can then think on higher levels and not have to worry about financial issues.

Normalization can also be bad because we can forget our foundational values and we can procrastinate and become complacent. We can also lose our focus on the basics because we've become elevated to such a high level of expertise that the early stages have become irrelevant. Yes, evolution is good and should be for the better; but, what if we're morally declining because we're deceived by a false belief? In his book, *Man's Search for Meaning*, Viktor Frankl, who was a concentration camp survivor of the Holocaust, recounts his experiences and notes how the victims grew apathetic to the insurmountably horrible situation. People adapted to the circumstances and started viewing their predicament as normal regardless of how inhumane and depraved it was. This is an outstanding display of how powerful our minds are with its ability to be conditioned and normalized.

> *"Yes, a man can get used to anything, but do not ask us how."*
>
> Viktor Frankl

This is why it is so important to regularly review your core values to see if what you're doing is in harmony with what you believe deep down inside you. It's very destructive to a person when they are a hypocrite and "living a lie" to themselves. This causes conflicts between the conscious and subconscious and an inner war is waged. This can become detrimental to emotional and mental health, leading to unhappiness and dissatisfaction even to the point of clinical depression. I've experienced depression for this very reason.

Pray for Your Enemies

Bless competition, don't curse them! Wishing evil or any other negative thing on your enemies and competition only floods your mind with more negativity. Whatever you curse, curses you. Rather, you should bless them and pray and wish them prosperity and abundance. You will be rewarded with evermore. This goes back to the principle of giving mentioned in chapter six, and the Law of Attraction mentioned in chapter two. When you give out life and love from your wellspring, you receive the like tenfold. When you sow toxicity and antagonism, you reap it back a hundredfold.

"What you resist persists."

Carl Jung

To focus your opposition on something that you're against only creates more of it! Why do you think when you force yourself into doing something by getting mad and thinking "I need to lose weight" or "I need to stop doing _____," it only ends up working against you and most of the time you end worst off than before? You need to focus on what you want, not what you don't want. Whatever you focus on is drawn to you, regardless of whether it is positive or negative. We live a self-fulfilling prophecy. Your subconscious mind is impersonal. It does not choose positive or negative. It only accepts what has been given to it by the conscious mind. We've used the techniques described in this book our whole lives, but now we are consciously aware of them. We can resolutely use them to our advantage. You must purposefully choose to have your subconscious mind to be filled with positivity by consciously dwelling on positive things.

"Finally, brothers and sisters, whatever is true, whatever is noble, whatever is right, whatever is pure, whatever is lovely, whatever is admirable—if anything is excellent or praiseworthy—think about such things."

Philippians 4:8

CHAPTER 9
DO NOW!

From Mind to Matter

You can set your thoughts on your goals and reprogram your mindset using destiny affirmations and dream conjurations all your life, but you will not achieve any of your goals until you act. Nothing happens until you take immediate action. There are no results without action. Renewing your mind prepares your mind to receive through action. Thinking is intangible and draws the tangible end goal to you but taking physical action steps is the only real way to take hold of that end-goal.

The Law of Cause and Effect is a law: if you sow positive, you reap positive, and if you sow negative, you reap negative. Easy enough. But it doesn't stop there. If you sow certain action (cause), you reap a certain result (effect). If you sow inaction (or incorrect action), you reap the appropriate result (usually not what you want). You don't plant corn and expect a wheat harvest. That isn't how the universe works. Jesus said it best, "A good tree cannot bear bad fruit, and a bad tree cannot bear good fruit" (Matthew 7:18).

> *"By thought, the thing you want is brought to you; by action you receive it."*
>
> Wallace D. Wattles

Put Your Plan Into Action!

Remember those plans you created earlier with the help of your subconscious mind? It's time to start doing the plans. A plan without execution is a wish, a wish that will never become anything and will disappear like your name and legacy if you don't actually take the steps included in the plan. Action, after all, is really the difference maker. You must act and act NOW! Don't talk your way out of it but *commit and do* without thinking how. You will figure it out. Remember, this is your destiny! You will never know if what you plan will work unless you try it out. You may fail, but failure, remember, is imperative to success. Failure is an indicator that what you are doing isn't the correct thing or you may simply just be going about it in the wrong way, and you need to *adjust*. Sometimes you may have to create an entirely new plan, but you won't know until you try your first plan.

There is no shortage of success, money, or accomplishment. Your level of success is in direct proportion to the amount of energy and action you put behind it. If you have a goal of $1 million, then you need (of course, goals and plans, but also) a certain amount of energy to achieve that goal. If you have a goal of $10 million, you will need to expend more energy. The same goes for $100 million, $1 billion, and so on and so forth. Your level of achievement relies on the amount of energy and action you are willing to put into it.

Progress is Action

To be successful, you must be continually progressing. When it comes to progress, there are only two directions to go: forward or backward. CHOOSE forward! Like I've mentioned before: if you think you're in neutral (because you're doing your *average*, everyday tasks, and work), you are actually in reverse. If you're not moving forward, you're moving backward. It's a common mistake for people to go on autopilot and think they are moving forward. This is because they want to settle for less and be comfortable, when in fact they could be far more comfortable in the end if they actually got outside of their comfort zone and did the things that others wouldn't dare to do (or the average person would be afraid to do because of the risk) and reap the massive rewards and success of getting uncomfortable and walking in confidence and faith.

Thinking you're moving forward but actually moving backward is like saving but not investing. If you keep your money in a savings account you can be fooled into thinking you're doing a good thing when in fact you are moving backward because at the rate of inflation you are actually losing money when you could be beating inflation and making a return (having your money work for you!) by investing that money rather than simply saving it. Assess constantly to assure yourself you are not moving backward. And if you've become complacent, stagnant, or whatever and moving backward and not forward, then figure out what you can do to start moving forward and do it. Do it now! Right at that moment get to the action.

Why Now! is the Only Time That Matters

Most people dwell in the past, many inhabit the future, but few live in the Now! You can choose to relive past experiences, but they won't get you anywhere because they cannot be changed. The past is done and gone, so don't waste your life there. You can live in the future, which is great and necessary for success, but we can get analysis paralysis which happens when we're caught up in planning and measuring so much that we procrastinate and don't do anything. The key place to be is *Now!* It's hard for us to do that because we assume we are living in the *Now!* (Which, in fact, we obviously are in the now—the present—but because of the complexity of our brains and the power of conditioned thinking we don't actually recognize the power of the *Now!* and living in the present.) We don't willingly exercise the *Now!* This is because we are caught up in what was or what could be and not what is. The *Now!* is where we have the most power, this is where our full power is exercised. This is where we act—*Now!* Act is in the present tense because this is a moment we can control.

You can think, affirm, and visualize as positively as you want, and you can work and put in as much energy and effort as you possibly can, but you will never be able to alter the past. The only thing you can do is change course NOW to prevent such past events from recurring in the future. (This principle of not being able to change the past applies equally with people. No matter how hard you try, you cannot change anyone else. You can only change yourself and how you react to other people's actions and attitudes.) *You can only create the future by taking action now!*

Unhappiness is the result of being anywhere but the present. Think about it: when you feel unhappy where is your mind at? You're either thinking about past events you cannot change and being upset about it (Victim Mentality), or you are thinking about the future of what you want instead of what you currently have and are upset and ungrateful for what you have now (Victim Mentality!) This is all outside of now, yet you are experiencing it in the now because you are reliving past experiences in the present moment and/or acting out future events that may or may not happen while in the present moment. You can have what you want, but you must act in the present moment instead of wasting the present by using the valuable time and power you have at the moment to think about the past or future.

The Power of Practice and Perseverance

"When I played with Michael Jordan on the Olympic team, there was a huge gap between his ability and the ability of the other great players on that team. But what impressed me was that he was always the first one on the floor and the last one to leave."

Steve Alford

You can have all the talent in the world and still be a poor nobody without practice. Stephen King, author, whose books have sold more than 350 million copies, once said: "Talent is cheaper than table salt. What separates the talented individual from the successful one is a lot of hard work." In the end, action, practice, and perseverance is what distinguishes greatness from mediocrity. You can be talented and still not be great. A lot of people are talented but not all those people are considered great or iconic. You have to hone your skill until you are made great. This takes self-discipline, and if you want to be a millionaire, you have to master yourself.

If you want to achieve anything of significance you are going to have to learn and master skills in the area you wish to excel in. There is no getting around this. If you are motivated enough by your goals and dream, then this shouldn't be a problem for you. That's why strong emotion and desire should be dominant in your affirmations and visualizations. Because when you read and speak your daily destiny affirmations, it should spark motivation and determination to achieve that which you want. Then you will be able to do whatever it takes to achieve those goals and dreams, no matter the cost or effort involved. If it doesn't fill you with emotion, then you should reassess your goals to determine whether they are what you *really* want.

I ask myself this question every day (you should, too): *How do I need to act now that matches who I want to be; how should I start talking like and thinking like?*

"Nothing in the world can take the place of Persistence. Talent will not; nothing is more common than unsuccessful men with talent. Genius will not; unrewarded genius is almost a proverb. Education will not; the world is full of educated derelicts. Persistence and determination alone are omnipotent. The slogan 'Press On' has solved and always will solve the problems of the human race."

Calvin Coolidge

IF YOU WANT TO LIVE THE LIFE YOU WANT TOMORROW, YOU HAVE TO LIVE THE YOU DON'T WANT TODAY!

That's what it's about: it's the grind—the HUSTLE! It's waking up early even when you don't feel like it. It's going to the gym even when you're tired. It's doing that extra set or those few more reps even when you're tired. It's going up to that person and asking that question even when you're scared. It takes going to sleep early even when all your friends are out there having fun and wasting money. It takes making meal preps and even eating the same thing every day to save those few extra bucks. It takes saying no to that cookie no matter how much it may be justified by you or anyone else in the moment to eat it. It takes not buying the latest and greatest and instead save that money to invest in something that will pay a hundredfold in dividends! Why? BECAUSE YOU HAVE A VISION, A PURPOSE AND A DESTINY!

Is It Worth the Risk?

"Progress always involves risk. You can't steal second base and keep your foot on first."

Frederick Wilcox

There is no reward without risk. You cannot afford to give in to fear and doubt if you want to be successful, you must take the risk. Life is full of uncertainties. The key to overcoming uncertainties is: if you are afraid, do it anyway. You don't have time to sit around and wait until the "right time." The "right time" will never come! Now is the right time. START NOW! Commit right this moment, don't wait, you'll figure it all out, you will find a way! Just take immediate and massive action!

"If you can't, you must; and if you must, you can."

Anthony Robbins

Everything you ever wanted in life is just outside of your comfort zone. You must be willing to step out of certainty and walk in uncertainty. It's time to live by faith. Faith, or belief, is the antithesis of fear. You must believe that you will succeed. You must take a step out onto the water. You'll never walk on water if you don't get out of the boat. Believe me: once you start walking on water, you'll be surprised how easy it is and how much of a myth the made-up feeling of fear was in your head. Before you know it, walking on water will become a normal and natural thing for you. You'll be running and dancing on water in no time! Soon, you'll be wanting to fly, and fly you will!

Why faith? Jack Canfield once said, "Most of us have never allowed ourselves to want what we truly want because we can't see how it's going to manifest." And that is the answer—the secret! When we really believe, expect, and then accept that we will have what we want, we can rest assured while our subconscious mind creates and works in conjunction with the universe to bring about opportunities that, if we accept and take on with action, will give us what we truly desire.

Can you do it? Sure you can. But do you really believe that? You must constantly reassess, challenge, and tweak your beliefs as often as necessary. Challenge everything, even everything you just read. Don't take my word for it; take your word for it. You'll never truly know if something is possible until you try. So, get out there and *Do Now!* Don't hesitate. Just commit and go for it!

"The biggest risk is not taking any risk ... In a world that's changing really quickly, the only strategy that is guaranteed to fail is not taking risks."

Mark Zuckerberg

MORE INFO

You can *Do Now!* by signing up for one of the Millionaire Mindset Now! Success, Investment and/or Entrepreneurship courses. Go to millionairemindsetnow.com/courses to sign up for one of our courses or one of our partner's courses. Don't forget to give this book a review and if you would like to contact me, feel free to email me any time at ben@millionairemindsetnow.com or ben@journeywithben.com I know you'll succeed whatever your goals are. I believe in you 1000%!

Much much love, Ben

Instagram: **@journeywithben**
Website: **journeywithben.com**

www.ingramcontent.com/pod-product-compliance
Lightning Source LLC
Chambersburg PA
CBHW021445210526
45463CB00002B/633